McGRAW-HILL SERIES IN MUSIC

DOUGLAS MOORE, CONSULTING EDITOR

BASIC
COUNTERPOINT

MCGRAW-HILL SERIES IN MUSIC

DOUGLAS MOORE, CONSULTING EDITOR

AtKisson, *Basic Counterpoint*
Chase, *America's Music*
Ratner, *Music: The Listener's Art*
Other titles in preparation

BASIC
COUNTERPOINT

Harold F. AtKisson

1956

McGRAW-HILL BOOK COMPANY, INC.
New York, Toronto, London

Preface

In writing this manual, which is designed for a one-year course, the author had several considerations in mind: (1) the presentation of the material from the sixteenth and eighteenth centuries which is of the greatest immediate and practical value to the student; (2) the construction of a text which concerns itself with terse explanation and direction only, in order to eliminate confusion; (3) the deduction of cause and definition of common denominator from the analysis of result, rather than the development of a separate rule for each result from the same cause; (4) the construction of a text which is in accord with sound, practical, and efficient pedagogical principles, principles based on available information concerning the function of the human *gestalt* in the learning process; those principles make imperative the reduction of the material to the smallest practical number of different frames of reference, or complexes.

Fux, in his *Gradus ad Parnassum*, 1725, attempted to classify the contrapuntal techniques into certain well-defined categories (species). Three of these are mentioned in Chapter 2 for want of better nomenclature. The third species (quarter notes against whole notes) and the fifth (combination of the first four), being completely erroneous in concept, are omitted.

The whole note *cantus firmus,* which has been a traditional part of contrapuntal pedagogy, has been of no practical value in the pedagogy of composition for centuries. Its use gives a false light to contrapuntal composition and retards the student's progress. It is, therefore, not used.

The use of the "C" clefs is an unnecessary burden in counterpoint study. They are not employed.

Any standard edition of the J. S. Bach *Two Part Inventions, Sinfonias,* and *Well Tempered Clavier* (first book) should be used to accompany the portion of this text which is concerned with eighteenth-century practices. The teacher might use to advantage any other supplementary material available to him.

Acknowledgment is made to three of my former teachers, T. Stanley Skinner for interest and inspiration, Gustave Fredric Soderlund and Allen I. McHose for much information; and to my students, whose searching questions prompted much effort.

Grateful acknowledgment is made to my good friend, novelist Lettie Rogers, for reading the manuscript when it was in longhand and to Elizabeth Cowling and Phillip Morgan for making sure that the examples the author wrote were devoid of parallel fifths and octaves.

Acknowledgment is also made to the Theory Faculty of the Department of Music, Columbia University, and to Mr. Donald White of the Eastman School of Music of the University of Rochester for many helpful suggestions; and to many others, whose names I do not know, who have read, commented, and thereby contributed.

HAROLD F. ATKISSON

Contents

Part One

Sixteenth

Century

Ecclesiastical

Style

*Part Two
Eighteenth
Century
Style*

Introduction

The definition of counterpoint (*punctus contra punctum*) is partially inherent in the name. It is the combination of notes (*puncti*) in certain and particular intervallic relationship to the lowest note of the combination. Chord structures are a result of the combination of voice lines.

The term counterpoint is often confused with *polyphony*, the combination of two or more equally important melodies. Polyphony is composed with contrapuntal techniques, but the techniques of counterpoint are not confined to polyphony. Homophony, a single melody accompanied by chords, may also be composed with contrapuntal techniques.

Harmony, as the subject has been traditionally approached, is the combination of notes related to a common fundamental and members of the harmonic series of that fundamental. Voice lines are usually generated from within the chord structures.

It would seem that the traditional approach to the study of harmony has come about, to some extent at least, as a result of the Rameau treatises of the early eighteenth century. Rameau, by experimentation, de-

1

fined the roots of the harmonic structures that were then in contrapuntal use. It would be difficult to gain a thorough comprehension of the art of musical composition if one confined his study to traditional, pedagogical harmony and did not examine the contrapuntal techniques from which traditional harmony evolved. The *long view* is essential. Though techniques may become ancient, they never lose their value either to the composer, performer, or listener.

Melodic structure is of primary concern in music written from either the contrapuntal or the harmonic point of view. The student is too often left to define for himself the essential features of a good melodic line. The harmonizing of an overly large number of given melodies and the fitting of Fuxian devices to a given *cantus firmus* consisting of whole notes often inhibits comprehension of melodic structure and, in many cases, any creative ability which may be within the capacity of the student.

That portion of a melodic line which should receive first consideration is the phrase, the musical sentence. All of the master composers have solved the problems of phrase structure either by intuition, experience, or study.

The phrase is composed of melodic motives (fragments) and may be of any length—classically of four bars which end with a cadence. Each phrase should contain a definite climax, which may be obtained either by elevation of the melodic contour (rarely depression) or by organization of the rhythmic structure so that the melody proceeds from short note values (sometimes a single short note value) to a longer value, creating an accent by duration. The two methods are often combined; in such a case the longer note value will appear at the highest elevation of the melodic contour. Syncopational distortions of the rhythm often create phrase climaxes, as do chromatic alterations in a melody line.

A variety of secondary climaxes are inherent in the structure of a longer phrase, but in each case one primary climax, or phrase point, should be outstanding.

In performance, a crescendo to the point of a phrase and a diminuendo from the point (the amount being within the realm of interpretation) creates the ebb and flow of which the listener is conscious when music is well performed. Misplacement of the phrase climax is sometimes desired by the composer, conductor, or performer, but great care must be taken lest the phrase sound clumsy and unmusical. The second example below is frequently distorted.

The works of any major composer are filled with numerous examples of phrases of all types which the student may examine at any time.

The combinations of phrases in larger organizations make up the various musical forms, some of which are discussed in later chapters.

The first two phrases of the Gregorian *Kyrie eleison* for feasts of the Blessed Virgin (*cum jubilo*) are excellent examples of the type of phrase climax which is produced by elevation of the melodic contour.

Ex. 1

Ky - ri - e _____ e - le - i - son __

As an example of the durational accent type of climax, the second theme of the fourth movement of the Tchaikovsky Fourth Symphony is very acceptable.

Ex. 2

The third movement of the Brahms *Trio in E♭,* Op. 40, offers an example of the combined melodic elevation and durational accent.

Ex. 3

The policy of the Roman Church toward liturgical music conditioned the melodic structure of the sixteenth-century ecclesiastical style to a great extent. The music serves a secondary role in the beautification of the words and is, therefore, subdued at times almost to the point of ambiguity.

The structure of the complete phrase (as opposed to the irregular, durational accent phrases that are discussed in the next chapter) is often of a type which gains momentum by the appearance of long note values near the beginning of the phrase, the phrase then proceeding into shorter note values as it extends. A primary climax by contour elevation, durational accent, or both, is usually found in the phrase. The following phrases are selected at random from the Palestrina Mass *Vestiva i Coelli.*

Ex. 4

Phrase structure in the works of J. S. Bach follows a similar pattern. In those used for polyphonic treatment, the climax is frequently placed near the beginning of the phrase so that the listener's attention will be called to any entry of the phrase in the polyphonic treatment.

The phrases sometimes follow a slow-fast-slow pattern with the smaller note values leading to a climax at the beginning of the last, slower portion. The following phrases are selected from Bach's *The Art of the Fugue.*

COUNTERPOINT I

Ex. 5

COUNTERPOINT III

COUNTERPOINT IX

The phrase structure in the following period (from a little minuet by Bach) makes use of typical phrase climaxes.

Ex. 6

The ecclesiastical modes, as presented in Chapter 1, use the later Greek names rather than the numerical designations of the Gregorian modes.

The dominants of the authentic Gregorian modes (modes 1, 3, 5, and 7, with finals on D, E, F, and G) were placed a fifth above the final, except that when the dominant encountered B, the note above, C, was used instead.

The plagal modes (2, 4, 6, and 8) used the same finals as the authentic modes (modes 1 and 2 used D, modes 3 and 4 used E, and so on) but the dominant in each plagal mode was placed a third below the dominant of the corresponding authentic mode, except that C was substituted for B in the plagal modes as it was in the authentic modes.

Early composers of modal melodies had such great difficulty in avoiding the tritone (augmented fourth) between F and B that it became known as the *diabolus in musica,* or the devil in music.

The student is cautioned that all of the information in this manual is cumulative in character, which is to say that every assignment for work within a style is a review assignment for all previous work within that style, as well as for practice in using the techniques and devices immediately involved. Later styles are modifications of, and contain additions to, earlier styles.

The student is further cautioned that a library does not contain a single idea. Marks on a page are meaningless within themselves and can only stimulate imagination. Visual symbolization of a functional description is essential if that function is to be comprehended. It does no good either to memorize rules for the sake of the rules or to substitute examples for mental effort.

"Study without thought is a waste of time, and thought without study is intellectual suicide," Confucius.

Sixteenth Century Ecclesiastical Style

Part One

1

Preliminary Considerations

Music in the Western World has until this century been organized around a tonic (or final) and a dominant.

Modal music used only one scale, the diatonic scale without key signature, with finals placed on the various notes of that scale. Dominants in sixteenth-century composition were, in theory, a fifth above the final in each case—as they were, in theory, in the Gregorian authentic modes—although the dominants were not always preferred cadence tones.

Cadence tones are those tones upon which a melody either ends or comes to rest. In the first few assignments it is the note upon which a melody ends (see Ex. 12, p. 16).

All of the modes except the Phrygian and Aeolian preferred the final and dominant as cadence tones. The Phrygian and Aeolian preferred the final and subdominant.

The closing cadence of a composition is always on the final of the mode. The use of other cadence tones is limited to interior cadences.

11

The modes used were

Mode	Final	Dominant	Preferred Cadence Tones
Dorian	D	A	Final, dominant, and mediant
Phrygian	E	(B)	Final, subdominant, and mediant
Lydian	F	C	Final, dominant, and mediant
Mixolydian	G	D	Final, dominant, and mediant
Aeolian	A	E	Final, subdominant, and mediant
Ionian	C	G	Final, dominant, and submediant*

Other cadence tones were used at times, but a knowledge of them is of more value to the musicologist than to the student of counterpoint.

In all of the modes except the Phrygian, the cadence tone is approached by semitone from below in one of the voices; the Phrygian used the whole step from D. Regardless of the number of voices, one of them must make the approach in that manner.

In the case of the cadences on G, A, and D, the step below was raised by accidental at the cadence to create the desired semitone approach. These accidentals (F♯, G♯, and C♯), along with B♭, were the only alterations of the diatonic scale commonly used. The lowered B was used in order to avoid the tritone (augmented fourth) between F and B in melodic skips and to avoid the leading tone effect when the melody sounded either A-B-A or G-B-A. F♯, G♯, and C♯ were infrequently used

---

* For a more detailed analysis of cadence tones consult either R. O. Morris, *Contrapuntal Technique in the Sixteenth Century*, London: Oxford University Press, 1922 , p. 15; or Gustave Fredric Soderlund, *Direct Approach to Counterpoint in 16th Century Style*, New York: Appleton-Century-Crofts, Inc., 1947, p. 15.

diatonically in the context of a composition. Chromatic use was very rare in the style and should not be attempted by the student. All of these alterations are known as false music, or *musica ficta*.

An essential feature of the style was the desire to maintain a balance between stepwise motion and skips in the melodic lines while avoiding melodic sequences. In half notes and larger values, stepwise, or scalewise, motion and skips were freely used.

A single skip might span any interval up to an octave, except the augmented fourth and the seventh; the sixth, being somewhat unvocal, appears infrequently. No distinction is made between major and minor intervals.

In half notes and larger values, a melody may skip twice in succession without changing direction, provided the *total* interval spanned by the two skips does not exceed an octave. The total interval is generally approached and left in contrary motion, as are other wide skips.

The rhythmic organization of sixteenth-century ecclesiastical music consisted of alternating heavy and light beats, or primary and secondary beats, which controlled the placement of cadences, passing and suspension dissonance, and rests.

The long note values (agogic accents) are balanced between the strong and light beats. Their irregular use results in irregular phrase lengths. The balancing of the agogic accents between the various voices results in interesting cross-rhythms, which are further accentuated by imitation and conditioned by the use of words.

Much of the music of the period can be barred in either $\frac{2}{2}$, $\frac{4}{2}$, or $\frac{6}{2}$ time, although bar lines were not used in composition. Some was written in triple time which, while interesting from the musicological point of view, does not greatly assist the student of counterpoint.

For pedagogic simplicity we shall use $\frac{4}{2}$ ($\mathlarger{\mathbb{C}}$) time in which the half note is the unit of the beat. The first and third beats are strong beats and the second and fourth are weak beats.

For practical purposes we shall use the double whole note, or brevis ($\mathbf{\bowtie}$), the whole, half, quarter, and eighth note values. The brevis may start only on beat one; the whole note may start on beats one, two, or three; and the half note on any beat; the dotted whole note may begin only on beat one. Quarter notes and eighth notes will be taken up at a later time.

When using bar lines, notes which extend over bar lines, which the sixteenth-century composer would have written as full note values, must be written as two values tied across the bar. The sum of the tied notes must be either a single note or a dotted note value; a note may be tied only to either a note of equal value or to a note of half the value of the first note. The same rule usually applies to repeated notes on the same pitch.

Ex. 8

Since the half note is almost never syncopated—
an exception will be noted later—quarter notes are
not tied across the bar line. Two, three, or four
double whole notes may be tied together.

At the beginning of a composition, voices start
either on a whole note or on a larger value, or on a
dotted half note followed by a quarter note (but do
not use the dotted half note until quarter notes have
been introduced). Cadences are always on strong
beats, and the final note must be a brevis if the cadence is on beat one or a whole note tied to a brevis
if the cadence is on beat three.

The most important single rhythmic device in the
style is what might be termed the *suspensional syncope*. No cadence is really complete without it. It
consists of either a whole note or a larger value which
produces a syncopation by being held over a strong
beat. It then moves downward by step on the following weak beat to either a half note or a whole
note.

Ex. 9

At cadences the syncope is held on the cadence
tone and resolves downward by step to a leading tone
(raised if F, G, or C) on the weak beat. It then moves
back to the cadence tone on the following strong
beat.

Ex. 10

When working on assignments in sixteenth-century style, write for soprano, alto, tenor, and bass voices. Use the treble clef for soprano and alto, the double treble (♭♭ sounding an octave lower than the treble) for the tenor, and the bass clef for the bass voice. The voice ranges were quite high for the bass and tenor in the sixteenth century, but for practical use in the present day the following ranges are recommended. They may, however, be modified.

Ex. 11

ASSIGNMENT   Using the information in this chapter and the following examples as models, write several modal melodies. Designate the voice and the mode. Be sure to maintain a balance in the use of steps and skips and in the variety of note values. Just as many whole notes should start on the weak beats as on the strong beats. Start on beat one on either the final or the dominant of the mode (final or subdominant in the Phrygian mode). ||

Ex. 12

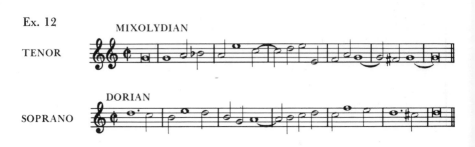

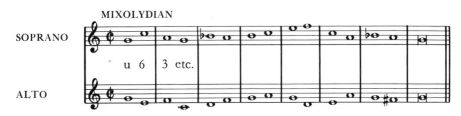

Ex. 14

and consonant intervals is called counterpoint in *first species.*

Analyze the harmonic intervals used in the following example and write one exercise with whole notes in the upper voice and half notes in the lower. Write a second exercise with the whole notes in the lower voice and half notes in the upper. Use the consonant intervals only and do not cross the voices.

When two notes are used in one voice against one note in the other, it is called counterpoint in the *second species.* ||

Ex. 15

1. PASSING DISSONANCE IN HALF NOTE VALUES: COMBINATION OF FIRST AND SECOND SPECIES

The passing tone used in half note values may appear only on weak beats (two or four). It must fill in a third and must proceed stepwise, without change of direction, from a consonance on a strong beat through the dissonant half note on the weak beat and to a consonance on the following strong beat. The addition of the half note passing tone completes the second species.

The neighboring tone in half note values should not be used.

Fifths and octaves separated by passing dissonance are considered to be consecutive.

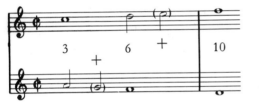

Ex. 16

ASSIGNMENT   Analyze the harmonic intervallic structure and passing dissonance and locate the agogic accents used in the following example. Indicate passing dissonance with a small plus (+) sign and agogic accents with an accent sign (∧).

Using the example as a model, write two exercises using second species (consonance and half note passing tones) freely in either voice. Skip only from consonance to consonance, and remember that the dot on a whole note, equal to a half note, must always be consonant with the other voice except when

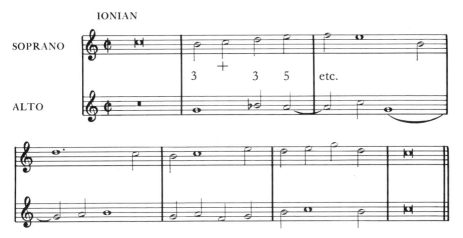

Ex. 17

it appears as a suspension dissonance (Section 2 of this chapter).

Do not write both exercises in the same mode. Maintain a balance of note values in both voices and between the two voices, and make sure that you have approximately the same number of agogic accents in both voices in order to ensure equality of importance. It is a good policy to alternate them between the voices in the first exercises. *Never allow the agogic accents* (long note values) *to start in both voices at the same time.*

Start one voice on either the final or the dominant (final or subdominant in the Phrygian mode) and on beat one, the other on either the final or the dominant and on beat three of the same bar or on beat one of the next bar. At the cadence the syncope should be used in one of the voices.

A note altered by *musica ficta* should never be doubled. *Musica ficta* should not be used in more than one voice at a time. ||

2. SUSPENSIONS

The suspension, of which three forms are used in two-part texture, is the only dissonance which may occur on the strong beat. In each instance the syncope, or suspension melody, prepares the dissonance on a weak beat. It is held over as a dissonance on the following strong beat and resolves downward by step on the next weak beat. The preparation, dissonance, and resolution must occupy at least three full beats; the preparation may occupy more than one beat.

The 2-3 suspension is the *only* one in which the suspensional syncope appears in the lowest voice. In the 7-6 and 4-3, the syncope is used in the upper voice.

The 2-3 suspension:

Ex. 18

The 7-6 suspension:

Ex. 19

The 4-3 suspension:

Ex. 20

Cadential Suspensions

No cadence is really complete without a suspension. The syncope starts on a weak beat as usual, but on the tone which is to be the cadence tone. The dissonance on the strong beat resolves downward by step to a leading tone (raised if F, G, or C) on the weak beat. It then ascends to the cadence tone on the following strong beat.

If you wish to cadence with the voices at the unison, use the 2-3 suspension in the lower voice. If you wish to cadence with the voices an octave apart, use the 7-6 suspension in the upper voice.

Ex. 21

Analyze the following example for harmonic content, passing dissonance, agogic accents, and sus-   ASSIGNMENT pensions. Using it as a model, write two short pieces using second species and suspensions freely in both parts. Be sure to use a suspension at the cadence in both of the pieces. ||

When you wish to end an exercise or composition, stop writing, leave a bar or two blank, and write in the cadence with its suspension; fill the vacant area with free counterpoint (any voice which is not performing a specific melodic function such as imitation is said to be in *free counterpoint*).

Suspensional syncopation and syncopation in consonance is called counterpoint in the *fourth species*.

Ex. 22

Ornamentation of Suspensions: The 7-6 with Change of Bass

Any suspension dissonance may be ornamented by resolving the suspension to a quarter note on the last half of the dissonance beat. The resolution must be repeated on the following weak beat in a larger

value (the portamento device). Although the composers of the sixteenth century avoided the use of
the simple portamento to a leading tone the student
may, for pedagogical simplification, make use of them
as he wishes.

Ex. 23

The portamento may be used either as a consonance or as an anticipation on the latter half of a
strong beat (very rarely on the latter half of a weak
beat). This is the only anticipation of any type used
in the style. It may appear in any voice. It must be
either prepared as a suspension or approached by
step from above.

Ex. 24

Lassus

Ex. 25

The bass may move to a consonance on the resolution beat of a 7-6 suspension by moving up a second, down a third, up a fourth, or down a fifth. The 7-6 suspension with a change of bass becomes the root-position seventh chord of later styles.

Ex. 26

The voice above a 2-3 suspension may move to any consonance on the resolution beat of the suspension.

Ex. 27

ASSIGNMENT   Write two exercises using these devices. ‖

3. CANON AND FREE IMITATION

Canon is a device of strict melodic imitation of one voice by another. The techniques are simple.

The repetition of the melody by the second voice may be at any interval from the first statement of the melody. If the same notes are repeated, it is called *canon at the unison.* If the melody is repeated either a second higher or a second lower than it appears originally, it is called *canon at the second* (above or below), and so on. If the leader (the first statement of the melody) begins on a strong beat, the follower (the repetition) must also begin on a strong beat. If the leader begins on a weak beat, the follower must also start on a weak beat.

When writing a canon, transfer the leader to the follower and write the leader to fit harmonically with the follower.

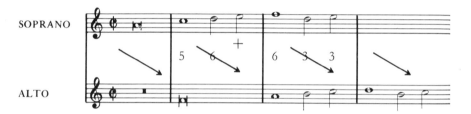

Ex. 28

Lassus

Ex. 29

The follower may be in augmentation (all note values doubled) or in diminution (all notes half the original value).

Write two canons. Use a different mode in each, and   ASSIGNMENT
imitate at a different interval in each. When you wish
to end, break the imitation and add a cadence. ||

Free Imitation

The composers of the sixteenth century used extended canon to some extent. Usually they imitated only the beginning, or head, of a theme, moving into free counterpoint after the statement or imitation. At the beginning, each voice imitates the preceding voice at the fourth or fifth, usually starting on either the final or dominant, and usually in exact imitation; however, an opening skip from the dominant to the final is often imitated by a skip from the final to the dominant, and vice versa (tonal imitation). Minor alterations of a melodic interval or a note value are permissible in the interior of a composition.

Imitation in contrary motion is not unusual. The theme appears upside down, or as it would appear in a mirror (mirror imitation). An ascending skip is imitated by a descending skip of the same interval, and vice versa.

Imitation is the binding force of all polyphony in all styles. Polyphonic forms are *fortespinnung* forms. They spin themselves forth.

ASSIGNMENT   Use the following example as a functional model and write two exercises, imitating the head of the theme in each exercise. Continue in free counterpoint for several bars before writing a final cadence. ||

Ex. 30

4. INTERIOR CADENCES: RESTS

The suspension is an essential feature of interior, as well as final, cadences. An added feature in interior cadences is the resting of the voices and the introduction of a new theme and its imitation. The preparation and suspension, resolution of the suspension downward by step to a leading tone, and the return to a cadence tone should *never be omitted from any cadence.* In interior cadences the cadence tone proper may be either a whole note or a brevis (rarely a value of six beats).

If the cadence tone is a whole note, the voice which does not have the suspension usually drops out as the cadence tone is sounded and re-enters with a new theme either before or as the cadence tone stops. The voice which contains the suspension and the cadence tone should rest immediately after the cadence tone. The rest must be of the same length as the rest in the other voice. The voice which held the cadence tone must then re-enter in imitation of the new theme. The new theme may enter on any beat and imitation may be at any interval. The new theme may start with quarter notes if four or more are used (Section 5 of this chapter). Infrequently the voice which does not have the suspension will be held through the rest in the cadencing voice, reversing the usual procedure.

The last note before a rest should be no smaller than a whole note and in any case should occupy an even number of beats. (A half note on a weak beat rarely appears before a rest.) Any rest *must* begin on a strong beat.

PHRYGIAN

Ex. 31

MIXOLYDIAN

Ex. 32

The use of B♭ as a signature is a common occurrence in music of the sixteenth-century ecclesiastical school. E♭ is used to correct the tritone and the use of G♯ is avoided.

Ex. 33

Ex. 34

If the cadence tone is a brevis in length, the voice
that does not have the suspension may drop out at
the start of the cadence tone; it must re-enter on the
second, third, or fourth beat of the cadence tone. If
the 7-6 suspension has been used, the second voice
may sound the octave with the first two beats of the
cadence tone and then drop out, rest one or two
beats, and re-enter with the new theme.

In any instance, the voice which has the suspension must sound the cadence tone and rest. The rests
should always be the same length in each voice in
two-part texture, and the re-entry should always begin with either a statement of a new theme or an imitation of a theme.

Ex. 35

Ex. 36

Write one composition in two sections. State and   ASSIGNMENT
imitate a new theme at the interior cadence, remem-

bering that interior cadences may be on any preferred cadence tone. The rules for starting and closing a composition remain the same. ‖

Rests

The primary purpose of a rest is either to call attention to the further imitation of the head of an old theme or the statement and imitation of a new theme. The use of rests for this purpose is not confined to interior cadences.

If the purpose of a rest is to call attention to the imitation of an old theme, it is not necessary for the rest to be repeated in the other voice; if it is for the purpose of calling attention to a new theme, the new theme must be imitated after a rest of the same length in the other voice. The last note before a rest should always be either a whole note or a larger value (rarely a half note). Only one voice may rest at a time, and the rests must begin on strong beats.

5. QUARTER AND EIGHTH NOTES

General Rules for the Use of Quarter Notes

1. The last quarter note of a passage of quarter notes, without regard to the number of notes involved, must appear on the last half of a beat.

2. Skip only from consonance to consonance, except when using the *cambiata* figure, and do not skip twice in succession without changing direction.

3. Any upward skip to a quarter note must be completed on the beat (the *high note law*). Downward skips are usually completed on the offbeat because of the requirement for consonance.

4. Any skip between two quarter notes must either

be approached in contrary motion or left in contrary motion. Skips may be approached and left in contrary motion.

5. Any skip between two quarter notes must either be approached by step or left by step. Skips may be approached and left by step.

6. All skips from a quarter note to a larger value must be made in contrary motion to the note preceding the skip.

Dotted Half and Single Quarter Notes

When only one quarter note is used following a dotted half note, the dotted half most frequently appears on a strong beat. The single quarter note then falls on the latter half of the following weak beat as a consonance, an unaccented passing tone, or a lower neighbor. A descending skip to a consonant quarter is permissible, provided it is left in contrary motion.

The dot on a half note (equal to a quarter note) must always be consonant with the other voice, except when it appears either as a suspension dissonance or against an accented quarter note passing tone.

The composers of the sixteenth-century period made it a general practice to sound a new note in the second voice on the beat when using a single quarter note on the latter half of that beat in order to preserve the rhythmic regularity.

Ex. 37

Aside from its use in the portamento figure, the single quarter note may appear on the latter half of a strong beat when the following note prepares a suspension.

Ex. 38

Quarter Notes in Pairs Only: Accented Quarter Note Passing Tones

Quarter notes in single pairs are generally used on weak beats.

If the second note ascends, the pair usually follows a half note and the entire figure is in ascending scale

line. The first quarter note of the pair must be consonant. The second may be either a consonance or an
unaccented passing tone.

Ex. 39

When the second quarter note of a pair descends,
the freedom of use is much greater. If the first quarter
note is consonant, it may be approached either by
step or skip. The second may then be consonant, a
lower neighbor, or an unaccented passing tone. A
descending skip to the second quarter note is permitted if it is consonant and the skip is approached
by step.

Ex. 40

Ex. 40 (continued)

In a descending scale line, the first quarter note of a pair may be an accented passing tone. The second must then be a consonance, which can be left by step in either direction or by an ascending skip.

Ex. 41

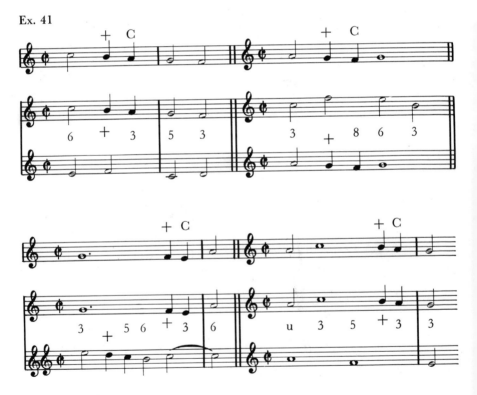

There is only one other form of the accented passing tone commonly used in sixteenth-century style.
When four quarter notes descend in scale line, the
third may be an accented passing tone. The next note
after the group of four quarter notes should ascend
by step and should be a larger value. Both the second
and third quarter notes of the group may be dissonant; if so, the first and fourth notes must be consonant. This (except for a similar figure in eighth
notes) is the only instance in which two consecutive dissonances were used in the entire style. An
accented passing tone may appear only on a weak
beat and only in descending form.

Ex. 42

Write one composition in two sections using single
quarter note pairs. You may use the accented passing tone. Remember that intervening passing dissonance does not remove the error from consecutive
fifths and octaves. || ASSIGNMENT

Extended Quarter Note Passages

Extended passages in quarter notes are used freely
in sixteenth-century style. They may begin on any

beat or half beat, but the last quarter note of a passage must be on the last half of a beat. They may change direction at will, although the composers of the sixteenth century usually avoided melodic sequences. The basic rules listed on page 32 must be observed.

Except for the two forms of the accented quarter note passing tone previously explained, *quarter notes on the beat must be consonant. Quarter notes on the off-beat may be consonant, passing tones, or lower neighbors.* The upper neighbor is rarely found. It is best used either to start a descending scale line or to end an ascending scale line.

ASSIGNMENT   Write a composition of two sections using extended quarter note passages. ||

Eighth Notes

Eighth notes are commonly used in single pairs only. They may appear on the last half of any beat. No skips to, from, or between eighth notes are permitted. One of the eighths—either one—must be consonant. If a single pair of eighth notes is used following a dotted half note, the second voice should move on the beat, as it should when the dotted half and quarter note figure is used, in order to preserve the rhythmic regularity.

Eighth notes in groups of four were very infrequently used in the style. Although they are not common, the student should have some experience in using them in order to prepare for the use of small note values in later periods.

They appear on any beat in scale line, or with

change of direction if desired, between half note and larger values only. One eighth note of each of the two pairs must be consonant. The second and third notes of the group may both be dissonant.

Ex. 43

The Ornamented and Extended Portamento Devices

The portamento may be ornamented with eighth notes in the manner shown in the following examples. Sometimes the ornamented portamento appears in augmentation (quarter notes instead of eighth notes).

Ex. 44

The portamento is frequently extended in only one manner, and the usual rules for the handling of eighth notes apply. The extended portamento is an idiomatic device which disappeared for all practical purposes after the sixteenth century.

Ex. 45

The following forms were infrequently used.

Ex. 46

ASSIGNMENT   Write a composition in two sections using the ornamented portamento and, if you wish, the common form of the extended portamento. ||

The Cambiata Figure

The only instance in which a skip from a dissonance may be employed in the style is embodied in the *cambiata*. The device consists of four notes. They progress downward a second, downward a third, and upward a second. The second note, which must be a quarter note on the latter half of a beat, may be a dissonance left by a downward skip of a third. The first and third notes must be consonant; the last note may be either a consonance or an acceptable passing tone.

Here are some possible forms.*

Ex. 47

*The classic form of the portamento makes use of the dotted half before the dissonance. It is recommended that the student be allowed the additional rhythmic freedom of the second and third examples.

6. THE SETTING OF WORDS

There are two basic rules for the setting of words evident in the music of the sixteenth century.

1. Generally, the smallest note value which may have a syllable of its own is the half note.

2. When a syllable is held over several notes, the syllable must close with either a half note or a larger value.

Several modifications of the basic rules are also evident.

1. The last syllable either before a rest or at a cadence should fall on the last note involved, without regard to other circumstances. The *alleluia technique* (the last syllable extended over many notes) is sometimes used.

2. Half notes may be divided into two quarter notes on the same pitch so that they may carry two syllables (infrequent). Whole note and larger values may be divided in like manner, provided the repetition is either of equal value or half the value of the first note.

3. Words of three syllables, which begin and end with strong syllables with a weak one between, may be set in the note values shown in the following example. Words of many syllables which begin with a similar syllabic arrangement may have the beginning ones set in the same note values.

Ex. 48

Aside from the rules and modifications listed, the use of words is subject to the application of a certain amount of common sense on the part of the student. Use the same placement of syllables in imitating, and make it a general practice to use strong syllables on agogic accents and when extending a syllable over many notes.

Each section of a composition should employ a complete sentence, clause, or phrase, and each voice must use the entire text of the sentence, clause, or phrase being set. Portions of the text may be repeated in one or all of the voices, but use prudence in doing so.

The declamatory style (one syllable for each note except eighth notes) may be used if your teacher permits.

Make a complete analysis of the following two-part   ASSIGNMENT
song. Indicate all consonant intervals and suspensions and mark all passing dissonance—passing tones, neighboring tones, portamento anticipations, and *cambiata* dissonance—with a small plus sign. Note carefully the themes and imitations. Letter each new theme as theme A, B, and so on. Note very carefully the use of words.

Set the following Latin text, a portion of the Ordinary of the Mass, in a composition of two sections.

Be-ne-di'-ctus qui ve'-nit / in no'-mi-ne Do'-mi-ni

Select a four- or five-line poem and set it to music. Use a new theme for each line, making sure that each line of your poem is a complete sentence, clause, or phrase. ||

Lassus

Ex. 49

tis - si - mi de -

al - tis - si - mi de -

pre - ca - bi - tur, de - pre-ca - - - -

pre-ca - - bi - tur, de - pre - ca -

- bi-tur de - pre-ca - - - - bi - tur.

- bi - tur, de - - pre - ca - bi - tur.

Ex. 49 (continued)

7. DOUBLE COUNTERPOINT

Double, or invertible, counterpoint is written in such a mathematical manner that the lower voice may be moved to the top and the upper voice moved to the bottom and the harmonic content still remain acceptable.

Double Counterpoint Invertible at the Octave

The simplest and most useful type of double counterpoint is that which is invertible at the octave. The lower voice may be moved up an octave so that it becomes the top voice, or the top voice may be moved down an octave so that it becomes the lower voice.

The techniques used in writing counterpoint invertible at the octave are quite simple. The prime inverted an octave becomes an octave, the second becomes a seventh, and so on, as shown in the following table. Note that upon inversion the 2-3 suspension becomes a 7-6, the 4-3 becomes a 5-6 (both intervals being consonant), and the 7-6 becomes a 2-3 suspension.

Intervals used when writing:	1	2	3	4	5	6	7	8
Appearance upon inversion:	8	7	6	5	4	3	2	1

Note also that the interval of a fifth inverts as a dissonant fourth and therefore cannot be used if the counterpoint is to be inverted at the octave. As long as the interval of a fifth is not used as a harmonic interval (it may be used as a passing dissonance) and parallel fourths (which invert as consecutive fifths) are avoided, all other devices and techniques of two-part counterpoint, including canon and imitation, may be used. The result will be invertible at the octave.

The techniques for recopying the completed product in inversion are also simple. Because of the problem of voice ranges, it is not usually practical in two-part writing to leave one voice in its original position and move the other voice an octave. The top voice may be moved downward and at the same time the lower voice may be moved upward. The same table as that shown above is used to determine how far

each voice may be moved. The upper voice may remain stationary and the lower voice move upward an
octave. The upper voice may be recopied a second
below its original position and the lower voice recopied a seventh higher, and so on.

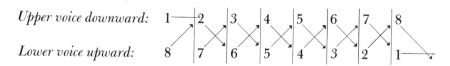

For practice, use the following example as a func-   ASSIGNMENT
tional model and write one exercise using counterpoint invertible at the octave from the beginning.
Imitate the theme. Write several bars, leave a bar or
two blank, invert the voices (using any of the combinations in the table), and recopy the lower voice on
the top stave and the upper voice on the lower stave.
Fill in the area left blank with free counterpoint and
add a cadence. ||

Ex. 50

Ex. 50 (continued)

Counterpoint invertible at the octave is the only form of double counterpoint that is practical for use in two-part texture. There are three other forms.

Double Counterpoint at the Tenth, Twelfth, and Fifteenth

Counterpoint invertible at the tenth can be used in a texture of two voices, but it is more practical for use in two voices in a texture of three or more parts. The harmonic intervals and suspensions which can be used may be ascertained from the following table. All tables are used in the same manner as the table constructed for counterpoint invertible at the octave.

1	2	3	4	5	6	7	8	9	10
10	9	8	7	6	5	4	3	2	1

Similar tables may be constructed for counterpoint invertible at the twelfth and fifteenth.

1	2	3	4	5	6	7	8	9	10	11	12
12	11	10	9	8	7	6	5	4	3	2	1

1	2	3	4	5	6	7	8	9	10	11	12	13	14	15
15	14	13	12	11	10	9	8	7	6	5	4	3	2	1

3

Three-part Writing

To state that the only difference between two- and three-part writing is the addition of a third part is not as naïve as it may appear to be. All of the rules for the handling of note values and the rhythmic placement of dissonance and cadences remain the same. At the beginning of a composition the voices enter separately in imitation, continuing as long as the composer wishes, or until the entrance of the third voice makes imitation too difficult.

As a general practice, the voices should not be separated from their nearest neighbor by more than an octave.

When notating intervallic relationships with Arabic numerals, call a tenth a third, a twelfth a fifth, and so on.

1. HARMONIC MATERIAL

The consonant intervals used in three-part writing are the same as those used in two-part composition. The intervallic relationship between the bass (lowest sounding voice) and each of the upper voices is the basis for harmonic structure.

49

Any combination of consonance above the bass may be freely used except the combination of the fifth and sixth, which requires special treatment. The intervallic relationship of the upper two voices to each other may be disregarded in combinations of consonance except for the avoidance of consecutive fifths and octaves and the approach to the unison.

The following example shows some of the possible combinations above a single bass note.

Ex. 51

A unison between any of the voices may be approached in contrary, or oblique, motion only. Octaves and fifths may be approached freely except for the avoidance of consecutives, but when they occur in similar motion between the outer (lowest and highest) voices, the upper voice must move by step and the lower by skip (avoiding covered fifths and octaves).

The only dissonances allowable on the beat are: the suspension used on a strong beat; and the half note passing tone, or the accented quarter note passing tone, used on a weak beat. Aside from these, the *beat must contain combinations of consonance and only combinations of consonance.* The harmonic structure may change at any time, but it is to be remembered that all moving voices, regardless of their number, must move in consonant relationship to the lowest moving voice.

For the best sound, the third or sixth should appear somewhere in each combination of consonance. Although combinations of perfect intervals are technically good, the sound is quite bare and open.

Either a root position or a first inversion triad structure will be implied by each combination of consonance.

2. PASSING DISSONANCE

The rhythmic control of the placement of passing dissonance that affects two-part writing also affects writing in three and more parts. A second voice may move with—or against—a passing dissonance in only one of two ways: (1) The second voice may move to a note which is consonant with both the passing dissonance and the third voice and has the rhythmic character of a passing dissonance; and (2) a second voice may move to another passing dissonance of the same note value as the first, if the interval between the two passing dissonances is a consonance. Two voices moving note against note (first species) while the third voice is held must move in consonant relationship to each other. All three voices may move at the same time only in combinations of consonance. Remember that a passing dissonance does not remove the error from consecutive fifths and octaves.

When writing three parts, notate with Arabic numerals only those intervals that are part of the combination of consonance (or triad structure) which involves all three voices. When two passing dissonances are used simultaneously, be sure that the interval between them is a consonance, but do not mark that interval with an Arabic numeral. Mark both passing dissonances with a plus sign to indicate that they are dissonant with the triad structure implied in the combination of consonance above the bass which immediately precedes the passing dissonance.

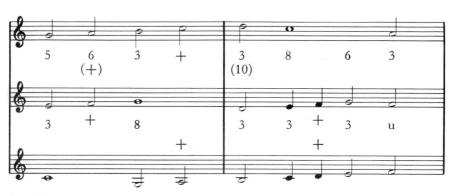

Ex. 52

3. SUSPENSIONS

The dissonant relationships of the suspension syncope are the same in three voices as in two. The added third voice moves freely through the suspension figure except on the beat of dissonance.

When either the 7-6 or 4-3 suspension is used, the third voice may sound any consonance above the bass except for that consonant interval which is involved in the suspension melody. (The sixth should not sound with the seventh in the 7-6, and the third should not sound with the fourth in the 4-3.)

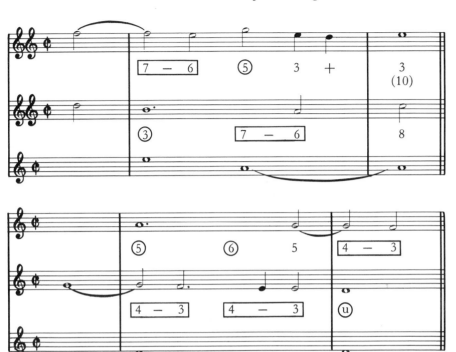

With the 2-3 suspension in the bass, the third voice may sound either a fourth, a fifth, or a sixth above the bass on the beat of dissonance. The third voice may move to any consonance upon resolution of the suspension.

Ex. 53

Ex. 54

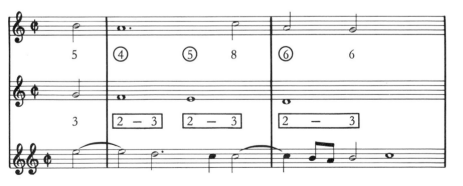

In three-voice writing, the 9-8 and 2-1 suspensions* may be used. With the dissonance of the 9-8,
the third voice may sound either a third or a sixth.
The open fifth is avoided.

Ex. 55

The third voice may sound either a third or a fifth
above the bass on the dissonance beat of a 2-1 suspension. The outer voices should not be more than a
fifth apart when the 2-1 is used. If the fifth is used
with the 2-1, the sonority is improved if the fifth
moves to another interval upon resolution of the suspension.

*The 9-8 and 2-1 suspensions are made possible by the use of 4-3,
7-6, and 2-3 suspensions between the two upper voices, with the bass
sounding the resolution tone. The 4-3 and 7-6 suspensions produce
the 9-8 under those circumstances, and the 2-3 produces the 2-1 suspension. Functionally they are 9-8 and 2-1 suspensions.

Ex. 56

Any two suspensions may be used simultaneously as long as the syncopes involved move in consonant relationship with each other.

Ex. 57

The change of bass may be used freely with the resolution of the 7-6, 9-8, and 4-3 suspensions. The bass may change to any note consonant with the resolution tone of the syncope.

Ex. 58

Upon the resolution of any suspension, the added third voice may move to any note that is consonant with the bass as long as the fifth is not used with the sixth. There are interesting possibilities for the use of quarter and eighth notes in the added voice.

4. FINAL CADENCES

Final cadences in all of the modes except the Phrygian employ a 4-3 suspension above the dominant. Both the voice containing the suspension melody and the bass move to the final. The third voice may sound any consonance except the third with the dissonant fourth of the 4-3 suspension. It then moves to the fifth on the resolution beat—or holds the fifth if it has been used with the fourth—and ascends to a third (or tenth) above the final on the cadence beat. The third voice may also move downward by step to the cadence tone, tripling the final. The tripled final is much more in the character of the early Netherland School than in the character of the sixteenth-century style.

If the third above the final is F, G, or C, it should be raised so that the final chord will contain a major third (*tierce de Picardie*).

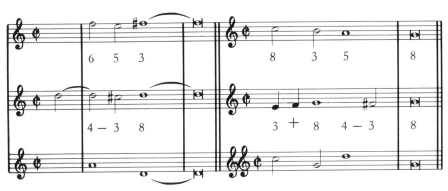

Ex. 59

Make a complete *harmonic* analysis (not a thematic ASSIGNMENT analysis) of the *Benedictus* by Palestrina which follows this assignment. You will notice that all three voices are in exact canon. This type of composition, which is difficult to write, is called *fuga*.

Write an exposition in three voices. Start the voices separately in imitation; keep the imitations exact as long as it is convenient to do so; continue in free counterpoint for several bars; and close with a final cadence. Use a separate stave for each voice, and start each voice on the final or dominant (final or subdominant in Phrygian), whichever is the more convenient for voicing. ||

MISSA: *Ad Fugam, Benedictus*   *Palestrina*

Ex. 60

Ex. 60 (continued)

The Phrygian Cadence

The cadence on E uses the 7-6 suspension above F.
The sixth (D) ascends to the final (E) on the cadence
beat as F descends. The third voice sounds the third
with the dissonance of the suspension and descends

to the raised third above the final on the cadence
beat.

Ex. 61

5. INTERIOR CADENCES

The essential feature of an interior cadence is the
suspension, its resolution to a leading tone, a return
to the cadence tone—which may be held two, four,
or six beats—and a rest. The suspension may be
either a 7-6, a 4-3, or a 2-3.

The voice with which the suspension is dissonant
(the base if either the 7-6 or 4-3 is used) should rest
while the cadence tone is sounding; the third voice
may rest at any time that no other voice is resting.
Only one voice may rest at a time, and all the voices
should re-enter after resting with either a statement
or an imitation of a new theme. The new theme may
enter in any manner acceptable in two-part writing.

It is not necessary that the rests be of equal length
in all the voices, although all rests should begin on
strong beats.

Aside from the demands of the interior cadence
that are listed, the voices may move in complete freedom within the scope of the style. Any attempt to

classify interior cadences as authentic, plagal, and leading tone cadences is, at best, pedantic.

It is not unusual for one of the voices to imitate an old theme at an interior cadence while the other voices are stating and imitating a new theme.

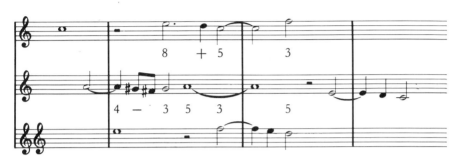

Ex. 62

The following example uses B♭ as a signature.

Ex. 63

The Phrygian cadence may be used on A by omitting the sharp from G and lowering B. The use of the Phrygian cadence is usually confined to the Phrygian mode.

ASSIGNMENT   Write a composition of two sections. State and imitate two themes. The interior cadence may be on any preferred cadence tone of the mode. ||

6. THE FIFTH IN COMBINATION WITH THE SIXTH

The $\frac{6}{5}$ is the antecedent of the first inversion seventh chord. It may be used only on a strong beat. The perfect fifth is prepared as a suspension and resolves downward by step as the bass ascends by step. The sixth may remain stationary, or it may move to another consonance upon resolution of the fifth. The downward resolution of the fifth may be ornamented in the same manner as a suspension.

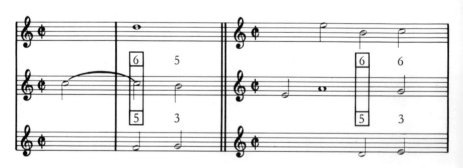

Ex. 64

The use of an accented passing tone will sometimes result in an unusual $\frac{6}{5}$. The $\frac{6}{5}$ thus created is a result and not a device. The composers of the sixteenth century sometimes used the fifth in combination with a prepared sixth, but the practice was unusual and should not be attempted by the student.

Write a composition of two sections, using the $\frac{6}{5}$ at least five times. ‖   ASSIGNMENT

7. FINAL CADENCE FORMULAS

The interval of a fourth above the bass may be used to prepare the cadential suspension. The cadential $\frac{6}{4}$ of later periods is a descendant of this practice. The fourth is introduced on a weak beat by step, and the bass is sustained. The third voice usually sounds the sixth with the fourth but may double the fourth (only on the weak beat) provided it approaches and departs by step. This device, called the consonant fourth, is sometimes used to prepare a 4-3 suspension within the context of a composition.

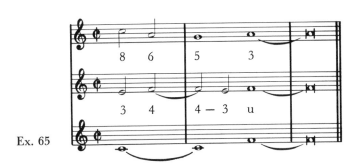

Ex. 65

The $\frac{6}{5}$ may precede the fourth. The bass is sustained on the dominant through the entire formula until it moves to the final.

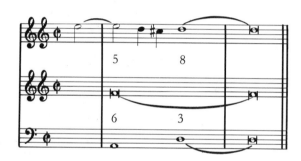

Ex. 66

The $\frac{6}{5}$ may replace the suspension. The resolution of the fifth is ornamented in augmentation on the resolution beat (rare).

Ex. 67

8. INVERTIBLE COUNTERPOINT AND CANON

Triple Counterpoint

Inversion at the octave is the only practical possibility in three-voice writing. The three voices may be exchanged in any manner. Avoid the fifth of the triad structure and parallel fourths, fifths, and octaves.

Two of the voices may be written in double

counterpoint invertible at any of the usual intervals with the third voice free.

Canon

Three-part canon is possible, though difficult, to write. A canon in two voices with the third voice free is much more common. This is one method of writing a three-part canon.

Each voice enters after an equal lapse of time. The middle voice is the leader. The lower voice, the first follower, is in canon at the octave below the leader. The leader continues in invertible counterpoint at the twelfth with the first follower, and fitting with the upper voice. The upper voice, the second follower, is the inversion at the twelfth of the leader and first follower.

Ex. 68

Other types of invertible counterpoint may be used in a similar manner. The student may experiment with them if he chooses.

ASSIGNMENT   Analyze completely the *Crucifixus* by Palestrina at
the end of this chapter.

Write a composition of two sections, using all of
the devices freely. Select one of the formulas for the
final cadence.

Set the following Latin text in a composition of
three sections. It is the *Kyrie* of the Mass. Make sure
that you repeat each phrase three times in each voice
in each section.*

Ky'-ri-e   e-lé'-i-son   (Use three times in each voice in section 1.)
(or *Ky-rie*) (or *e-lei-son*)
Chri'-ste   e-lé'-i-son   (Use three times in each voice in section 2.)
Ky-ri-e   e-le-i-son   (Use three times in each voice in section 3.)

Choose a short poem and set it to music. Use one
line in each section. ‖

---

*Sixteenth-century ecclesiastical composers usually used a final ca-
dence at the close of each portion of the *Kyrie*, beginning the following
section as a new composition. The form assigned above is used to give
the student experience in using the interior cadence.

MISSA: *O Regem Cœli, Crucifixus*   *Palestrina*

Ex. 69

Ex. 69 (continued)

Ex. 69 (continued)

Ex. 69 (continued)

Ex. 69 (continued)

4

Writing in Four and More Parts

The addition of a fourth part, or more as the case may be, is a matter of little additional technical difficulty, but avoidance of consecutive fifths and octaves does become increasingly difficult as more parts are added.

The techniques of imitation remain the same. However, the greater the number of parts, the greater the amount of freedom that may be exercised in imitation and the use of rests, although rests should still begin on strong beats and the note before the rest should still contain an even number of beats. The primary purpose of a rest is to call attention to imitation of some type, without regard to the number of voices in the texture.

1. HARMONIC MATERIAL

The combinations of consonance used in three-part writing are the basis for all harmonic structures. Doubling is either at the convenience or at the necessity of the movement of the voice lines although, for the sake of sonority, either the third or the sixth should appear in each combination. The following

example shows some of the intervals and doublings
that might occur over a single bass note.

Ex. 70

2. SUSPENSIONS AND THE $\frac{6}{5}$

Suspensions are used in the same manner as in
three parts. The combination of intervals above the
bass on the beat of dissonance is the only problem
for consideration.

With the 7-6, any consonant interval except the
sixth may be used in a third voice. The fourth voice
doubles any voice except the one which contains the
syncope. The third and fifth may be used together to
fill in the root-position seventh chord. The bass may
change upon resolution of the suspension.

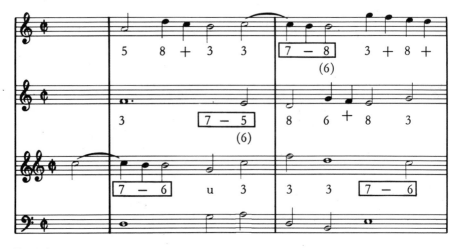

Ex. 71

With the 4-3, any combination of consonance which does not contain the third may be used. The bass may change.

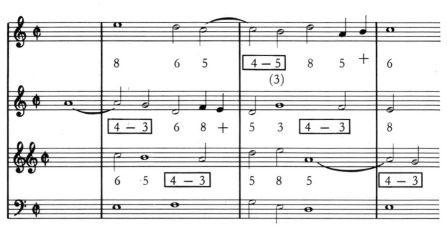

Ex. 72

With the 2-3 suspension, the fourth, fifth, or sixth may be used in a third voice. The remaining voice doubles any note except the syncope. The fourth and sixth may be used to fill in the third inversion of a seventh chord.

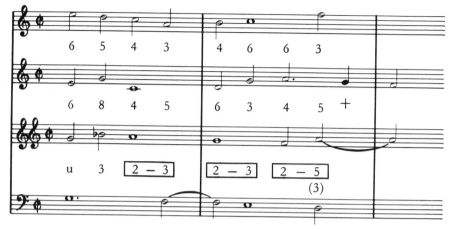

Ex. 73

The 9-8 and 2-1 suspensions may employ either a third or the third and fifth. The bass may change when the 9-8 suspension resolves.

The $^6_5$ may have the sixth doubled but may not have the bass doubled at the unison. Either the third or the octave, or both, may be used. The addition of a third to the $^6_5$ completes a first inversion seventh chord.

Ex. 74

3. PASSING DISSONANCE

The rules for the use of passing dissonance remain the same. Any number of voices may contain passing dissonance at the same time. The note values should be the same, the rules for the placement of dissonance must be observed, and the moving voices must be in consonant relationship with the lowest moving voice. Consecutive octaves and fifths must be avoided.

Ex. 75

4. CADENCES

Final cadences employ the same techniques and formulas as in three-part writing. The rules of doubling on the beat of dissonance are described in Section 2 of this chapter. The final chord may be a complete root-position triad.

Interior cadences and rests follow the three-part pattern. It is permissible for two voices to rest at the same time if only for a few beats. As a general rule, only one voice should rest at a time.

5. QUADRUPLE AND QUINTUPLE COUNTERPOINT AND CANON

The rules for writing four- and five-part counterpoint invertible at the octave are the same as those used in three-part writing. Avoid the fifth of the triad structure and parallel fourths, fifths, and octaves. For obvious reasons all of the possible arrangements of the voices are never used in one composition.

A canon between two of the voices in multivoiced compositions is practical and is frequently used. Canon in three or more parts, with other voices free, is not only difficult to write but is somewhat impractical as well.

Make a complete thematic and harmonic analysis of ASSIGNMENT the following portion of the *Kyrie* from Palestrina's *Virtute Magna* Mass.

Write one exposition in four voices. Close with a final cadence.

Write a *Benedictus* in four voices (page 43).

Set to music a short poem of your choice.

Whether or not you will be asked to write in five or more voices is left to the discretion of the teacher. ||

MISSA: *Virtute Magna, Kyrie*   *Palestrina*

Ex. 76

Ex. 76 (continued)

Ex. 76 (continued)

5

Some Aspects of Composition in the Seventeenth Century

The seventeenth century was a century of invention, experimentation, and revision of concepts in the fields of modality and tonality, instrumental music and the opera.

A trend which had existed in secular music in the sixteenth century toward the use of the Ionian (major key) and the Aeolian (minor key) modes as the basis for composition became well established in all music.

*Musica ficta** was used not only to create a leading tone at cadences, but to lend variety to the melody lines and chord structures as well. The insertion of *musica ficta* alterations into the texture could, either by the introduction of a new leading tone or by the destruction of an old one, introduce a new key.

The major mode used the raised C, F, and G and lowered B (♯1, ♯4, ♯5, and ♭7) in the key of C.

*The use of the term *musica ficta* instead of *chromatic alteration* is a technical anachronism, used to preserve the frame of reference as well as to preserve the historical continuity in this and following chapters.

Other major keys were transpositions of the mode, and the altered tones were placed in the same relationship to the tonic in which they appear in the key of C major (Ionian mode).

Ex. 77

One *musica ficta* alteration was added. The lowered sixth (♭6) was sometimes used in conjunction with ♭7 in descending scale lines. The ♭6 was also used—but infrequently—in the same manner as the lowered B in sixteenth-century style (5-♭6-5 and 4-♭6-5). The augmented second between 7 and ♭6 was avoided. The chromatic approach to any lowered tone was rarely used.

Ex. 78

It is to be remembered that the Aeolian (minor) mode made use of the same *musica ficta* alterations as in the sixteenth-century style. The raised F and G became the ♯6 and ♯7 in the key of A minor. The raised C became ♯3 (the *tierce de Picardie* was frequently used) and the lowered B became ♭2. The first inversion of the triad on ♭2 came to be known as the *Neapolitan sixth*.

A Minor

Ex. 79

In sixteenth-century style, the cadence on the dominant of the Aeolian mode (E) was avoided; the Phrygian cadence was usually confined to the Phrygian mode. The emergence of the Aeolian mode as a minor key, *per se,* demanded a cadence on the dominant. This necessitated the addition of the raised D (♯4) to create a *musica ficta* leading tone to the dominant. The ♯3 and the ♯4 may be used together in moving to a cadence on the dominant, or ♯3 and ♯4 may become ♯6 and ♯7 in the *key* of the dominant.

A Minor

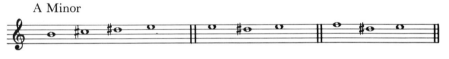

Ex. 80

The general use of the leading tone in the minor mode to maintain the key was essential, although the unaltered seventh and sixth of the minor scale (natural minor) were frequently used in descending scale lines. The ♯6 and ♯7 (melodic minor) were used together in ascending scale lines; they rarely appear together in extended descending lines. The augmented second between 6 and ♯7 was avoided.

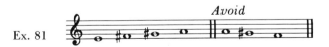

Ex. 81

In all minor keys, the altered tones were placed in the same relationship to the tonic as those in A minor.

A Minor   C Minor

Ex. 82

Leading tones in minor were approached freely by step or skip and could be left by step to the tonic or by skip to another member of the implied harmonic structure in which it was used. Other alterations were approached either by chromatic or diatonic step or by a descending skip—if to a raised tone.

All altered tones, except for the harmonic skip from the leading tone, resolved by step in the direction of the alteration as in sixteenth-century style.

The "high note law," already disappearing from sixteenth-century secular music, was abolished. The unprepared 7-6 suspension above the *dominant* (allegedly first used by Monteverdi) made its appearance, bringing the dominant seventh chord into the compositional picture.

The $^6_5$ was often used in conjunction with the $^6_4$ at cadences in much the same manner as it was used in the sixteenth century (page 63). In the seventeenth century the $^6_5$ was more frequently used above the subdominant. It then moved either to a $^5_3$ over the dominant or to a $^6_4$ over the dominant—if on a strong beat—which moved to a $^5_3$ over a sustained bass. Even though the bass skips an octave, it is still

considered to be sustained. The similar formula of
the sixteenth century, which appeared over a sustained dominant throughout, is occasionally observed
in music written as late as the eighteenth century.

The anticipation of the cadence tone as used in the
following example is a popular replacement for the
cadential suspension.

Ex. 83

Solo writing for the voice and the newly perfected
stringed instruments demanded new concepts of
composition. In that field polyphony was forced to
give way to contrapuntal homophony.

Listen to some recordings of solo music for the
violin by Corelli. It can be noticed that a florid solo
in the soprano voice is accompanied by a comparatively simple bass, which is constructed according
to the rules of two-part counterpoint, with simple
combinations of consonance and a few suspensions
(usually with change of bass) used as a filler between
the bass and the florid soprano. In the written music,
the filler was usually indicated only by numerical figures placed above or below the bass note to indicate
the desired intervals above the bass (*basso continuo* or
thorough bass). Some passages in block combinations
in first species were also used. The *basso continuo* ac-

companiment was employed with duets and trios as well as with solos.

The *basso continuo,* which is an outstanding device of the Baroque period as a whole (roughly from the death of Palestrina to the death of Bach), usurped from the leading tone a considerable amount of importance in the cadence function. The skip from the dominant to the final in the bass was used in previous centuries quite obviously because it happened to fit with the leading tone to tonic motion at the cadence. In the Baroque period, the downward skip of a fifth, or the ascending skip of a fourth, in the bass from the dominant to the tonic is of greater importance than the leading tone to tonic motion.

When listening to music of the Baroque period, you will notice the frequency of such bass lines as these at the cadences. They imply subdominant, or supertonic, harmonies that move to the root-position dominant, and thence to the tonic harmony. The leading tone in the dominant harmony does not always move to the tonic.

Ex. 84

These practices characterized, generally, the instrumental and solo music of the period. Polyphony had, however, not given ground where vocal groups were concerned, although the madrigal and motet were altered to some extent. The words were made to follow as nearly as possible the natural inflections of the spoken language (*stile rappresentativo*).

Set several lines of poetry in the Ionian mode (key of C) freely using *musica ficta* as outlined previously in this chapter. You may modulate to any closely related key (F, G, A minor, or D minor) by introducing the leading tone of the new key as a *musica ficta* alteration, or by using ♭7 to create the key of the subdominant. The key of E minor may be obtained through G major. The new key is maintained only as long as the alteration is used.

Write in $\frac{4}{4}$ time and reduce all sixteenth-century note values by half—the eighth note becomes a sixteenth, and so on. *All rules for the rhythmic placement of dissonance and the combination of voice lines remain the same.*

Start either in imitation or with two voices in free counterpoint proceeding into imitation. Write for three or four voices. ‖

Eighteenth Century Style

Part Two

6

Two-part Writing: The Two-part Invention

The various aspects of evolution in polyphonic music from the sixteenth and seventeenth centuries to the eighteenth are embodied almost in entirety in the Bach *Two Part Inventions.* As one becomes more familiar with sixteenth- and eighteenth-century music the similarities begin to seem much greater in number than the differences.

The principles of imitation are much the same as in the sixteenth century. The basic difference is that eighteenth-century polyphony usually exposes and develops a single theme in one composition. Themes range from single motives (thematic fragments) to extended melodies composed of several distinct, yet cohesive, motives. The *Inventions* run the gamut.

The imitation is usually at either the unison or octave at the beginning, with free imitation at any interval, inverted or not, following. The purpose of the composition is to expend completely the musical value of the theme.

The *Inventions* are written for instrumental performance; thus the limitations in regard to melodic skips are withdrawn, except for augmented intervals.

Note values are the same as those used in the previous chapter (sixteenth-century values reduced by half). Some consideration should be given, however, to the tempo. At a very fast tempo, the functions of the values might revert to the functions of the sixteenth century. At a slow tempo, the eighth note may take on the function of the quarter note, and so on.

Sixteenth notes may skip freely from consonance to consonance. The thirty-second note may be used on the weaker portions of the beat. They usually replace either the last or the last two semiquavers (sixteenth note values).

Repetitions on the same pitch may be longer than the note repeated.

Rests should be preceded by no value smaller than an eighth note (rarely a sixteenth note).

Harmonic intervals are fundamentally the same. The fourth may be used, however, in small note values, provided it is composed of the fifth and root of an implied triad. One voice should either move to the fourth by skip of a third from the third of the implied triad, move immediately a third to the third of the implied triad, or move a third to an appoggiatura (page 96). The implied triad is not syncopated.

Bach

Ex. 85

Implied harmonic structures take on considerable importance. The tonic and dominant chords are by far the most frequently used. *Invention 1* is made up of implied tonic and dominant harmonies almost to the exclusion of all others.

The dominant seventh chord has emerged as a harmonic structure; the added subdominant in the dominant chord is not considered to be a suspension. The seventh of the dominant seventh chord (the subdominant) may sound with any other member of the chord, producing either consonance or dissonance. The seventh should resolve downward by step, with or without ornamentation. Arpeggiation in sixteenth notes up to the ninth above the dominant has been observed in two-part texture.

Musica ficta may alter the harmonic intervals freely, except for the creation of augmented intervals and major sevenths above the bass, but should not be used in both voices simultaneously. After a new key has been established, the accidentals used to indicate and maintain the new key are not *musica ficta* (chromatic alteration).

Musica ficta alterations, except the lowered seventh, may be approached by either chromatic or diatonic step or by a descending skip. The lowered seventh in major (and the lowered sixth) may be approached either by diatonic step or by an ascending skip of a third. The chromatic approach is infrequently used.

Leading tones, including the *musica ficta* leading tone in minor, may be approached either by step or by skip in either direction. They should be left either by step to the tonic or by skip to another member of the implied harmonic structure. Leading tones may descend by step as a result of scalewise pressure.

Otherwise, *musica ficta* resolves by step in the direction of its alteration.

Avoid augmented intervals and major sevenths when using musica ficta.

The suspensions used are the same as those used in sixteenth-century style, however much greater freedom in preparation and resolution is allowed.

As a general rule, suspensions which employ quarter notes, or larger values, should appear on strong beats if the change of bass is not used. If the change of bass is used, they are likely to appear on any beat. In triple time, they may appear on any beat with, or without, a change of bass.

Suspensions which employ eighth note values should appear on the beat without change of bass, or on any half beat with change of bass.

Generally, the preparation of a suspension should not be of shorter value, or time duration, than the duration which elapses between the establishment of the dissonance and the actual resolution of that dissonance.

Once a suspension dissonance has been established, any voice not involved in the suspension syncope may move freely within the implied triad, or seventh chord, structure.

Suspension ornamentations are the same, with three types added. The resolution may be ornamented by the skip of a third from the dissonant note of the syncope. The voice then moves by step to the resolution. They may also be ornamented by a descending skip to a member of the implied chord structure and an ascending skip, or step, to the resolution; or by a changing tone figure.

Ex. 86

In polyphony, Bach preferred to use the suspension on strong beats, as had the sixteenth-century ecclesiastical composers. All of the types mentioned were used quite freely in Bach's *basso continuo* writing (chorale harmonization, etc.) but almost all of those used in polyphonic writing are found on the strong beats without regard to whether or not the change of bass has been used. The following examples are representative of their use in two-part texture.

Ex. 87

The rhythmic control of the placement of passing dissonance remains fundamentally the same. The first and third semiquavers (sixteenth note values) of the beat are considered to be the strong portions of the beat.

One of each pair of sixteenth notes moving stepwise on a half beat should be consonant (the same rule that governed the use of eighth notes in sixteenth-century style).

Bach

6 + + 3   Ex. 88

A skip to a dissonance on the second or fourth semiquaver of the beat is permitted, provided the dissonant sixteenth note is left either by step to a consonance or by step to an accented (on the beat or half beat) sixteenth note passing tone (appoggiatura).

Bach

3 + 5 6   Ex. 89

It is permissible to skip in contrary motion to a consonance from a dissonant sixteenth note on either the second or fourth semiquaver of the beat (escape tone). The dissonance should be approached by step.

Ex. 90

Appoggiaturas and escape tones infrequently appear in sixteenth note values on strong portions of the beat or in eighth note values on the latter half of a beat.

After a semiquaver rest on the beat, the second and third semiquavers of the beat may be dissonant if they are in scale line.

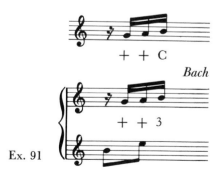

Ex. 91

To the two familiar forms of the accented passing tone in eighth note values (quarter note values in Chapter 2) one is added. An upper neighbor returns to an accented passing tone; a lower neighbor rarely returns to an ascending accented passing tone. Two simultaneous eighth note accented passing tones are rarely found within the framework of a dominant seventh chord structure (*Sinfonia 1,* bar 12, beat 4, J. S. Bach).

Ex. 92

The same figure appears, moving freely in either direction, in sixteenth note values. The device is infrequently syncopated.

Ex. 93

The changing tone figure is frequently encountered as a melodic device as well as a suspension ornamentation. A neighboring tone skips to the opposite neighbor before resolving.

Ex. 94

The portamento anticipation is frequently used in sixteenth as well as eighth note values. The figure is usually approached by step—infrequently by skip— and was quite often used to anticipate the cadence tone on the preceding weak beat, or preceding half beat. The portamento anticipation sometimes appears in the ascending form in sixteenth note values.

Bach frequently used two types of passing dissonance simultaneously which were not in consonant relationship to each other. When used, they generally appear in sixteenth note values on either the second or fourth semiquavers of the beat. One is a passing tone, the other an appoggiatura resolving to a consonance. The appoggiatura may appear as a chord tone moving to an accented sixteenth note passing tone (*Sinfonia 1,* bar 6, beat 2). Simultaneous sixteenth note passing tones on the third semiquaver of the beat are not infrequent.

When writing scalewise triplet figures, in either simple or compound meters, one note of the group of three should be consonant. The first should be either a consonance or an accented passing tone.

Except for the practices described, all note against note (first species) writing must be in thirds, fifths, sixths, and octaves. Avoid consecutive fifths and octaves whether they be either directly parallel or on consecutive beats or consecutive half beats.

The student is referred to the work of C. P. E. Bach (see bibliography) for a complete listing of eighteenth-century ornamentations and some possible nonharmonic tones which may result from such ornamentations.

Entire portions of the texture (usually a bar) may be recopied at a higher, or lower, pitch if the "ends" are smoothly joined (sequence). Sequences are sometimes moved from the tonic to the dominant (with or without change of key) but usually appear either a second or a third higher or lower and in the original key. A sequence may be repeated several times, provided it moves the same diatonic interval each time. The sequence should not be overused.

Final cadences are of the root position dominant to tonic chord type. The use of suspensions and anticipations is optional. The composers of the period sometimes used the 4-3 suspension in the cadence chord. The raised third in the final cadence chord in minor keys is also optional.

The fourth above the bass may be used in conjunction with the sixth immediately preceding the cadential dominant chord. It usually appears on a strong beat. The fourth descends.

The $^6_5$ over the subdominant moving to either a $^5_3$ or a $^6_4$ over the dominant is more popular as a cadence formula than it was in the seventeenth century. (Listen to some recordings of violin solo music by Tartini.) These chords—which became the II $^6_5$, I $^6_4$, V, and I chords—are frequently implied in two part cadences.

All cadences, both final and interior, *are primarily dependent upon the dominant to tonic motion of the bass line* as discussed in the previous chapter. A short rest after such motion helps to lend emphasis to an interior cadence.

ASSIGNMENT   Make a complete aural and written analysis (including thematic usage, keys, and implied harmonic structures) of *Inventions 1* and *2.* Note carefully the development of the principal themes and the use of *musica ficta* in modulation. Modulation through *musica ficta* (chromatic alteration) creates possibilities of *musica ficta* alteration in the new key, although such possibilities are seldom exploited. Note carefully the interior cadences.

Examine the presentation of the theme at the beginning of all of the *Inventions*. Observe carefully the use of syncopation in *Invention 6*. You will find that some of the *Inventions* are based on two motives instead of a complete phrase.

Write several themes of the character of those used. Select the two you think best and write an invention on each. Develop the theme by constant free imitation of all types, including inversion, or even diminution and augmentation. Imitate the melodic contour or rhythmic pattern in places where you cannot use other types of imitation. The separate motives may be used as well as the entire theme, but under any circumstances you should use as little free counterpoint as possible.

Introduce by *musica ficta* alteration at least three different closely related keys aside from the tonic in each invention. Use two or three interior cadences in related keys.

Do not double either the leading tone or any tone altered by musica ficta and avoid cross-relationships. ||

7

Three-part Writing: The Sinfonia

Imitation at the beginning of a sinfonia usually alternates between the tonic and dominant keys. The soprano states the subject (theme) with the bass providing an accompaniment in free counterpoint. The alto imitates in the dominant key as the soprano provides a countersubject (countermelody). The bass then restates the subject in the tonic key after dropping out for several beats. In some of the sinfonias, the alto imitates in the tonic key, and in others the bass does not state the theme at all in the exposition.

After the exposition of the theme in all of the voices, the theme and its motives are developed as in the *Two Part Inventions*. The countersubject and the bass accompaniment to the first statement of the theme may or may not be used in developing the subject.

ASSIGNMENT Analyze carefully the thematic material used in all of the *Sinfonias* of Bach. Note any deviation from the above description. ||

Harmonic structures are based on the same combinations of intervals that were used in the sixteenth century. The combination of the fifth and sixth is not nearly as frequently used as it was in previous centuries, except in the harmonization of chorale melodies. The fifth of the $\frac{6}{5}$ is treated in the same manner as a suspension dissonance. The fifth need not be prepared if it appears as the seventh of a dominant seventh chord in first inversion. Combinations of intervals above the bass using only perfect intervals are generally avoided.

The *Sinfonias* are not at all chromatic in character. The simultaneous use of *musica ficta* in two voices was avoided. It is to be remembered that accidentals used to maintain a key are not *musica ficta*.

The usual three voice suspensions are employed. However, the type of freedom that Bach allowed himself in some instances did not, as a general rule, seem to extend to the treatment of the third voice in suspensions.

Any of the consonant intervals could be used with the suspension dissonance except for that consonant interval involved in the syncope—by edict of tradition. Even so, he preferred to use the third with the 9-8 and 7-6 suspensions and the fifth with the 4-3 and most frequently held those added consonances until the suspension resolved. The fourth was preferred with the 2-3 suspension in the bass.

Ex. 95

One voice may momentarily double the dissonant note of the syncope on the weak portion of the half beat.

Although in polyphony Bach preferred to use the 7-6 in an implied first inversion chord and the 9-8, 4-3, and 2-3 suspensions in implied root-position chords, the traditional possibilities should not be discounted. Any of the intervals used with the various suspensions in the preceding centuries are established by tradition and might be used. Furthermore, the fact that Bach preferred to hold the added note until the suspension resolved does not discount the traditional possibility of freely moving any voice not involved in the syncope after the dissonance has been established.

There is one departure from, or readaptation of, tradition which Bach sometimes employed with the 7-6 suspension. The prepared seventh is used with the fifth. The bass moves downward a third to the root of an implied ninth chord. The fifth becomes the seventh of a 7-6 suspension which resolves in the traditional manner, and the seventh, now a ninth, ascends by skip to the fifth of the implied ninth chord. Bach used this device twice in *Sinfonia 1* (bars 4 and 8). Analyze both.

Ex. 96

Aside from the techniques for the use of sixteenth notes outlined in the previous chapter, the rules which govern the use of passing dissonance in three-voice writing are fundamentally the same as in previous centuries. Except for the rules mentioned, voices moving in first species should move in consonance.

In compositions in three or more voices, a repeated chord tone, with or without embellishment by neighboring tones, is not considered to be a moving voice except for the avoidance of consecutive perfect fifths and octaves.

Aside from the accented dissonance which has been described, combinations of consonant intervals above the bass should be used on the beat.

ASSIGNMENT Make a complete thematic and harmonic analysis of one of the *Sinfonias*. Attention to key and implied chord structure is essential.

Examine the thematic development in all of the *Sinfonias*.

Write a sinfonia patterned on those of Bach. ||

8

Four-part Writing: The Fugue

Anyone who has learned how to write three-voice counterpoint has, at the same time, learned to write in four or more voices. The same combinations of consonant intervals above the bass are used. Either the third or the sixth should be present in any chord structure or enter by suspension resolution.

1. CHROMATICISM

The simultaneous use of *musica ficta* (chromatic alteration) in two voices, as well as its use in a single voice, is a practice frequently employed in eighteenth-century writing. The frequency and scope of the employment were dependent upon the degree of chromatic color desired. Doubling of *musica ficta* and the leading tone was avoided, as were cross-relationships.

Major Keys

One new alteration is added—the lowered third of the scale—which may appear in major keys as a passing tone, or in combination with another *musica ficta* alteration.

In effect the use of ♭6 and ♭3 makes the minor key chords available for use in the major mode. A change of mode by the use of ♭3 in the tonic chord was, however, avoided.

Any combination of two *musica ficta* alterations is acceptable as long as the combination results in either a major, minor, or diminished triad, or any of those triads with a minor or diminished seventh added as a suspension, as the fifth of a $^6_5$, or as the seventh of a dominant seventh chord. The triads and seventh chords that are implied may be used in root position, first inversion, or third inversion. There is no traditional background for the second inversion.

The augmented triads, seventh chords with an augmented triad or major seventh, and chords containing other augmented intervals were avoided. One exception is noted: the lowered sixth may appear in the bass simultaneously with the raised fourth of the scale (♭6 and ♯4) in an upper voice. This combination of alterations results in chord structures that later became known as the *chords of the augmented sixth*.

The ♯1, ♯4, ♯5, ♭7, ♭6, and ♭3 are all available for use either singly or in combinations of two alterations. The maintenance of a chromatic scale line takes precedence over the normal directional departure from *musica ficta* alterations. The student is cautioned that he should not confuse accidentals used to maintain a key with *musica ficta*.

Minor Keys

In minor keys the simultaneous use of *musica ficta* in two voices is limited to the use of the raised fourth of the scale in the bass in conjunction with the raised sixth degree in an upper voice. Infrequently the raised fourth degree is used in an upper voice with the unaltered sixth tone of the minor scale in the bass (chord of the augmented sixth).

The lowered second degree is found, but rarely, above the subdominant in the bass in an implied major triad in first inversion (Neapolitan sixth). The augmented triad based on the third degree of the scale and containing the *musica ficta* minor key leading tone was used infrequently. When it appears, it is usually in first inversion, avoiding the augmented fifth above the bass that would occur in its root position.

Only the ♯4 and ♯6 were used in combination.

Because of the fact that the *musica ficta* used in the relative major and minor keys springs from a common ancestor, it sometimes becomes exceedingly difficult to define the exact point at which the minor keys and their relative major keys meet, or the exact point at which a composer has left a minor key and modulated to its relative major.

2. THE FUGUE

Analysis of result without attention to cause has led to much misunderstanding of the fugue form. Some analysts accept the idiomatic use of the form by a single composer as being the form itself.

The fugue is descended from imitation as practiced in the Netherland School (from Ockeghem and Obrecht to Palestrina, or ca. 1430 to ca. 1600). Basically it consists of two sections, the exposition of a theme and the development of the exposed theme. Any attempt to formulate a list of hard and fast rules to govern the content and thematic employment can be countered by an equally impressive list of instances in which those rules have been broken. There are certain practices which are general and for which there is a background of tradition.

The Exposition

A fugue theme, or subject, is a complete phrase beginning on either the tonic or the dominant— rarely the mediant—and ending with a cadence on either the tonic or the dominant tones of the scale. If the cadence is on the dominant, the *musica ficta* leading tone may or may not be used. Sometimes the cadence is on the mediant in an implied tonic chord.

Fugue subjects may be classified according to the type of answer (imitation) that is given to them by the second entering voice. These imitations, or answers, are either *real* or *tonal*.

A real answer is an exact repetition of the subject in the key of the dominant (infrequently the subdominant). A real answer is given a subject that does not move between the tonic and dominant tones of the scale either at the beginning or at the end, or during the subject by modulation.

Subject   *Bach*

Ex. 97

Ex. 97 (continued)

A tonal answer is given a subject that moves between the tonic and dominant tones of the key, or vice versa. Such motion is given an answer that is adjusted so that the dominant tone will stand in the answer at the same rhythmic point at which the tonic tone stands in the subject, or vice versa. The positions of the tonic and dominant tones are reversed; the melodic contour remains the same.

Most tonal answers can be classified according to the location in the subject and answer of the tonic-dominant motion, or according to whether or not modulation is present.

TONAL, TYPE I

A subject which modulates from the tonic key to the dominant key is imitated by an answer which modulates from the dominant key back to the tonic key, or vice versa.

In both of the following examples you will notice that motion in the subject from the tonic (C) to the dominant (G) is imitated by motion in the answer from the dominant tone of the tonic key (G) to the tonic (C).

Ex. 98

Ex. 98 (continued)

TONAL, TYPE II

A subject that opens with motion between the tonic and dominant of the key is usually imitated by an answer which opens with the reverse of that motion, but with the same melodic contour. A dominant to tonic skip is answered by a tonic to dominant skip, or vice versa. Sometimes a considerable amount of embellishment is found between the tonic and dominant tones, requiring adjustment to be made in the answer in a manner that will enable the reversed tones to appear in the same rhythmic locations in which they appear in the subject. The rhythmic structure and melodic contour remain the same.

The tonal answer of a tonic-dominant motion results in a dominant-tonic motion in the answer. This appearance of the tonic tone in the answer necessitates an adjustment of the answer into the key of the dominant at the first convenient point.

Infrequently, a subject of this type is given a real answer.

J. C. Bach

J. S. Bach

Ex. 99

Ex. 99 (continued)

TONAL, TYPE III

Some subjects are found, particularly in the fugues of Buxtehude, which contain motion from the dominant to the tonic note and then proceed back to the dominant, with or without modulation. Such subjects may be considered to be a compounding of tonal types I and II. The reverse motion should appear in the answer, arranged in a manner that will allow those reversed tones to be placed at the same rhythmic locations in which they appear in the subject.

Ex. 100

The nature of the tonal answer demands a certain degree of freedom in its construction. Adjustments should be made at points of convenience and musical good taste. A slight change in the size of an interval skip is not as readily noticeable as the use of either a repetition or a skip in the answer where none existed in the subject. Adjustment into the key of the dominant in the type II tonal answer should occur as soon as musical possibility permits.

In the exposition the subject is stated first. The statement may occur in any of the voices. The answer may enter either before the subject ends, or a few beats afterward, or as the subject ends. The first voice continues with a countermelody (countersubject). As additional voices enter, they usually alternate between the subject and the answer and continue with free counterpoint, which may or may not be used in the development section. An episode (material inserted between regular statements of the subject and answer—often a sequence based on a motive from the countersubject) may be inserted at any time after the first answer. Once a voice has entered, it usually does not rest until the end of the exposition (the number of voices is the composer's choice).

After the last voice has made its statement, the exposition may either end immediately or close with an episode. The fugue may be extended in length by further exposition (counterexposition).

An irregular exposition is not at all uncommon. The very first fugue in Bach's *Well Tempered Clavier,* book one, is an excellent example of a fugue which has an irregular exposition.

In the following exposition, it can be noticed that the voice which first stated the subject drops out during the exposition and re-enters with the statement of the subject that ushers in the development section. It can also be noticed that Bach introduces the first rhythmic motive of the subject as a countersubject.

J. S. Bach

End of exposition

Ex. 101

Analyze the expositions of at least six of the fugues
in the *Well Tempered Clavier*, book one, and examine and classify the subjects and answers of all of
the fugues in the book.

Write several fugue subjects of each type and
write answers for each. Expose at least one of each
type in three or four voices. ||

Development

The content of a development section ranges from
regular statements of the subject with sequential episodes interspersed to free imitational development
as in the *Inventions* and *Sinfonias.*

The development may employ the countersubject
stated with the first appearance of the answer (regular countersubject) or new countersubject material
may be introduced at the beginning of the development (irregular countersubject). Several countersubjects may be stated and exploited in episodes during
the development.

Development sections frequently open with a
statement of the subject in the key of the tonic. A
new countersubject may or may not be introduced
with it.

Statements of the subject and answer may be made
in a variety of *musica ficta* introduced keys, in augmentation, diminution, and inversion. Regular statements may be interspersed between episodes and
free imitation of the subject, countersubject, or motives from either. Free, or exact, imitation of the subject in *stretto* (entrances closely overlapping) is often
used—usually in the latter portion of the development.

In short, the only limitations of ways and means of

using the subject and countersubject, or countersubjects, are the limitations of the composer's ability to find ways and means.

The number of voices employed may vary, but do not destroy the linear aspect of the composition with a large number of short rests. It is to be remembered that the voice line is of paramount concern in polyphonic music. A rest is an excellent method of calling attention to a coming entry of the subject or answer (a sixteenth-century technique).

Fugues often close with a statement, or free imitation, of the subject in either the key of the tonic or the dominant, frequently over either a tonic or dominant pedal point. (The dominant or the tonic may be introduced, most frequently in the bass, as a consonance and sustained. The first voice above takes over the normal function of the bass in harmonic structures. The pedal point ends as a consonance.)

The use of either tonic or dominant pedal points in other voices with a statement, or free imitation, of the subject is not infrequent. In the final bars the fugue often gathers momentum by the use of more extended scalewise passages and the use of smaller note values.

The return to a statement, or imitation, of the subject in either the key of the tonic or of the dominant has led some analysts to label the fugue as a ternary form. It may appear to be so, but the appearance comes about quite by accident. A ternary form, as generally considered, makes use of two themes. The fugue develops only one.

Some fugues are found in which a second subject is substituted in place of the answer and both of the subjects are developed. This type of fugue, which is comparatively rare, is called a *double fugue*.

Make a thorough thematic analysis of at least two   ASSIGNMENT
fugues from the *Well Tempered Clavier,* first book. Locate all subject and countersubject material and ascertain the number of different countersubjects that are introduced and exploited in each. The re-copying of a fugue using colored pencils is very valuable. Use one color for the subject and its imitations, a different color for each different countersubject, and black for free counterpoint. There will be a surprisingly small amount of black when the copying is completed.

Make a complete thematic and harmonic analysis of the following fugue. It has been selected because of the clarity of its structure. The regular countersubject is quite distinctive and its employment in the development section is readily discernible.

Write a fugue in four voices. ||

J. S. Bach

Ex. 102

Ex. 102 (continued)

Ex. 102 (continued)

Ex. 102 (continued)

Conclusion

If class time permits, there are several forms which should be given consideration in any extension of a counterpoint class beyond the material presented in this manual, but they are left to the devices of the teacher for the sake of brevity. The madrigal and motet from the early period and the organ chorale, *chaconne* and *passacaglia,* and the toccata from the Baroque period are among those that should receive attention.

If time does not permit the classroom study of those forms, the student may consult any standard reference volume for explanations and descriptions. The contrapuntal techniques are similar in all works of the same period.

The complicated polyphony of the eighteenth century, coupled, perhaps, with the treatises of Rameau, resulted in a compositional revolution toward music much more simple in construction.

The move toward simplicity and frivolity brought about a style adapted from the homophony of instrumental solo music and the opera *recitativo* and *aria.* It consisted of a frivolous melody which said little and a very simple chordal accompaniment which said less. The style was called *empfindsamkeit, style galant, simplicité, rococo,* and *zopf* (pigtail) music. The style developed through Stamitz and the Mannheim School into the classic forms of Haydn and Mozart.

Although the polyphonic forms were occasionally employed by composers of later periods and the techniques used to some extent in the development sections of other forms, the *fortespinnung* art has never achieved the position in later times that it held up to and including the eighteenth century.

Composers of the twentieth century, having to some extent exhausted the possibility of greater variation and individuality in the use of harmonic techniques, are again experimenting with the polyphonic forms. The primary characteristic of twentieth-century polyphony is not only its freedom of rhythmic structure in the voice lines, but considerably greater freedom in harmonic construction as well.

Bibliography

Apel, Willi: *Harvard Dictionary of Music.* Cambridge: Harvard University Press, 1950.

Apel, Willi: *The Notation of Polyphonic Music, 900–1600.* Cambridge: The Mediaeval Academy of America, 1949.

Arnold, F. T.: *The Art of Accompaniment From a Thorough-Bass.* London: Oxford University Press, 1931.

Bach, C. P. E.: *Essay on the True Art of Playing Keyboard Instruments,* trans. and ed. by William J. Mitchell. New York: W. W. Norton & Company, Inc., 1949.

Bach, J. S.: *Complete Organ Works.* New York: G. Schirmer, Inc., 1913.

Bach, J. S.: *Gesellschaft.* Ann Arbor: J. W. Edwards, Publisher, Inc., 1947.

Boyden, David D.: *A Manual of Counterpoint,* vol. I. Berkeley: University Extension, University of California, 1946.

Bridge, J. Frederick: *Double Counterpoint and Canon.* London: Novello and Co., Ltd., 1881.

Buxtehude, Dietrich: *Samtliche Orgelwerke.* Copenhagen: Wilhelm Hansen, 1952.

Cherubini, L.: *Counterpoint and Fugue,* trans. by Mary Cowden Clarke, ed. by Joseph Bennett. London: Novello and Co., Ltd., n.d.

Fux, Johann Joseph: *Steps to Parnassus,* trans. by Alfred Mann. New York: W. W. Norton & Company, Inc., 1934.

Goetschius, Percy: *Counterpoint Applied.* New York: G. Schirmer, Inc., 1902.

Haupt, August: *Counterpoint, Fugue, and Double Counterpoint,* trans. by H. Clarence Eddy. New York: G. Schirmer, Inc., 1876.

Jeppeson, Knud: *The Style of Palestrina and the Dissonance.* London: Oxford University Press, 1946.

Kitson, C. H.: *The Art of Counterpoint.* London: Oxford University Press, 1907.

Kitson, C. H.: *Counterpoint for Beginners.* London: Oxford University Press, 1937.

Kitson, C. H.: *Studies in Fugue.* London: Oxford University Press, 1928.

Krenek, Ernest: *Studies in Counterpoint.* New York: G. Schirmer, Inc., 1940.

Lasso, Orlandi De: *Complectens Omnes.* Monaco: Nicolai Henrici, 1604.

Liber Usualis. Tournai (Belgium): Desclee and Co., 1947.

Lytle, Victor Vaughn: *The Theory and Practice of Strict Counterpoint.* Philadelphia: Oliver Ditson Co., 1940.

McHose, Allen Irvin: *The Contrapuntal Harmonic Technique of the 18th Century.* New York: Appleton-Century-Crofts, Inc., 1947.

Merritt, Arthur Tillman: *Sixteenth-Century Polyphony.* Cambridge: Harvard University Press, 1939.

Morris, R. O.: *Contrapuntal Technique in the Sixteenth Century.* London: Oxford University Press, 1934.

Oldroyd, George: *The Technique and Spirit of the Fugue.* London: Oxford University Press, 1949.

Orem, Preston Ware: *Manual of Fugue.* Bryn Mawr: Theodore Presser Company, 1939.

Palestrina, Giovanni Pierluigi Da: *Le Opere Complete.* Rome: Edizione Fratelli Scalera, 1939.

Pearce, Charles W.: *Modern Academic Counterpoint.* Boston: Boston Music Co., n.d.

Pearce, Charles W.: *Students' Counterpoint.* New York: G. Schirmer, Inc., 1926.

Piston, Walter: *Counterpoint.* New York: W. W. Norton and Company, Inc., 1947.

Porter, Quincey: *A Study of Sixteenth Century Counterpoint.* Boston: New England Conservatory of Music, Second Edition, 1942.

Prout, Ebenezer: *Double Counterpoint and Canon.* London: Augener, Ltd., 1891.

Prout, Ebenezer: *Fugal Analysis.* London: Augener, Ltd., 1892.

Prout, Ebenezer: *Fugue.* London: Augener, Ltd., 1891.

Reti, Rudolph: *The Thematic Process in Music.* New York: The Macmillan Company, 1951.

Richardson, A. Madeley: *Fundamental Counterpoint.* New York: American Book Company, 1930.

Richardson, A. Madeley: *Helps to Fugue Writing.* New York: The H. W. Grey Co., 1930.

Ruffer, Joseph: *Composition With Twelve Notes,* trans. by Humphrey Searle. New York: The Macmillan Company, 1952.

Sachs, Curt: *Our Musical Heritage.* New York: Prentice-Hall, Inc., 1949.

Sachs, Curt: *Rhythm and Tempo.* New York: W. W. Norton and Company, Inc., 1953.

Schweiger, Hertha: *A Brief Compendium of Early Organ Music.* New York: G. Schirmer, Inc., 1943.

Soderlund, Gustave Fredric: *Direct Approach to Counterpoint in 16th Century Style.* New York: Appleton-Century-Crofts, Inc., 1947.

Soderlund, Gustave Fredric: *Examples of Gregorian Chant and Works by Orlandus Lassus, Giovanni Pierluigi Palestrina and Marc Antonio Ingegneri.* New York: Appleton-Century-Crofts, Inc., 1946.

*Musical
Examples*

Appendix

BENEDICTUS

Lassus

CANTUS: Be - - ne - di - ctus _____ qui ve - - - - - - nit in no-mi - ne _____ Do - - - mi - ni, in no-mi - ne, _____ in no-mi - ne, _____ in no-mi - ne _____ Do - - - mi - ni.

TENOR: Be - - - ne - di - ctus _____ qui ve - - nit in no-mi-ne Do - - - - - - - mi - ni, in no-mi - ne, _____ in no-mi - ne, _____ in no-mi - ne _____ Do - - - - mi - ni.

CANTIONES

MASS: *Repleatur Os Meum Laude, Benedictus*   *Palestrina*

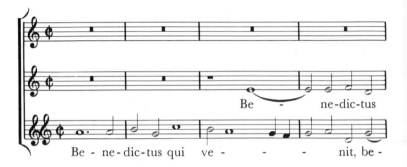

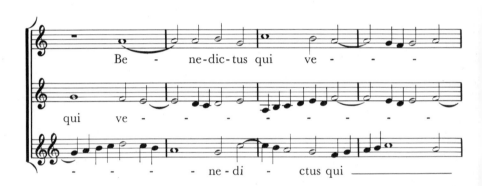

143

MOTET: *Dies Sanctificatus*

Palestrina

145

de - scen - dit lux ma - gna in ter - ris; haec ___

ris; ___ haec

ris, lux ma - gna in ___ ter - - - ris;

ma - gna ___ in ter - - - ris; haec

___ di - es guam fe - cit Do - - -

di - es guam fe - cit Do - - mi - nus, guam

haec di - es,

di - es,

- - - mi - nus, ___

fe - cit Do - mi - nus, haec di - es ___ guam fe - cit

haec ___ di - es guam fe - cit

haec ___ di -

(Declamatory Style)

150

151

MOTET: *Vox in Rama*

Clemens Non Papa

152

153

154

MASS: *L'homme Arme, Sanctus* — *Palestrina*

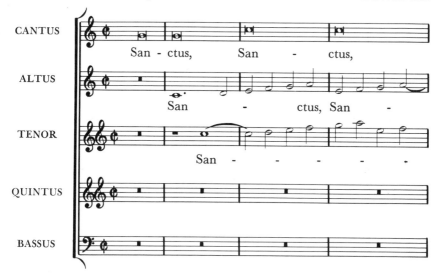

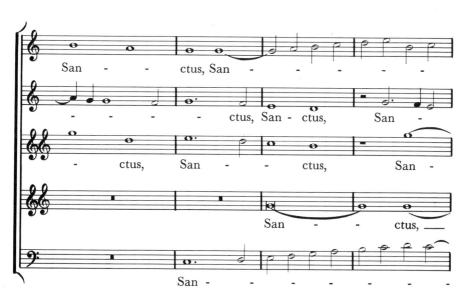

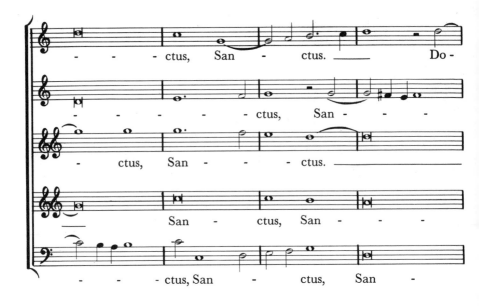

Do - mi - nus De - us Sa - - ba -

oth, _____ Do - mi·nus De - us,

- ba - oth, Do - mi - nus De - us Sa - ba - oth, _____

- mi - nus

- us Sa - ba - oth, ____

oth, Do - mi - nus De - us, Do -

Do - mi - nus De - - us Sa - ba -

Do - mi -

De - us _____ Sa - -

Do - mi - nus De - us Sa - ba -

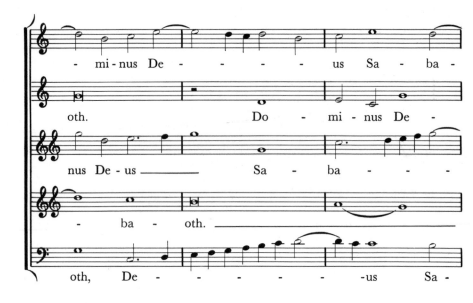

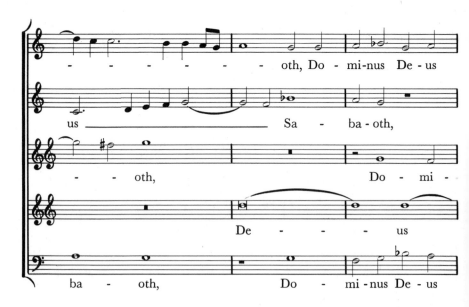

160

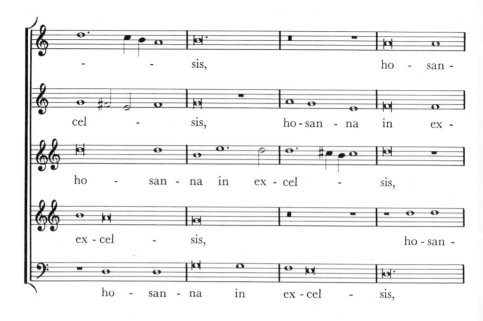

- - sis, ho - san -

cel - sis, ho - san - na in ex -

ho - san - na in ex - cel - sis,

ex - cel - sis, ho - san -

ho - san - na in ex - cel - sis,

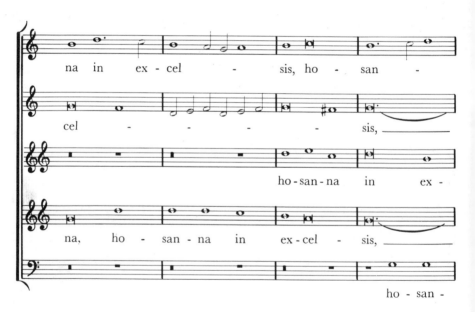

na in ex - cel - sis, ho - san -

cel - sis, _____

ho - san - na in ex -

na, ho - san - na in ex - cel - sis, _____

ho - san -

na in ex - cel - sis, in ex - cel -

___ in ex - cel - sis,

cel - - - sis,

___ ho - san -

na, ho - san - na in ex - cel - sis,

- sis, ho - san - na

ho - san - na _____ in ex - cel -

ho - san - na _____

na in ex - cel - sis,

ho - san - na in ex - cel -

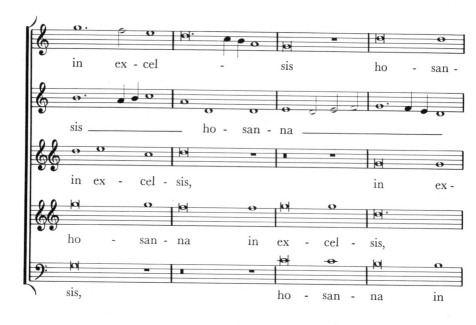

in ex - cel - sis ho - san -

sis _____ ho - san - na _____

in ex - cel - sis, in ex -

ho - san - na in ex - cel - sis,

sis, ho - san - na in

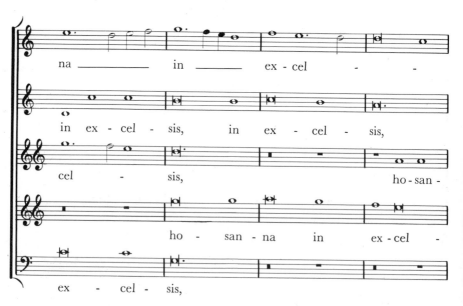

na _____ in _____ ex - cel - -

in ex - cel - sis, in ex - cel - sis,

cel - sis, ho - san -

ho - san - na in ex - cel -

ex - cel - sis,

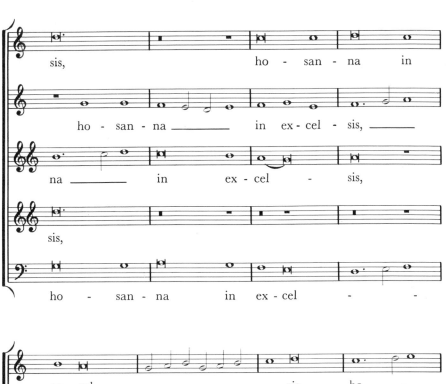

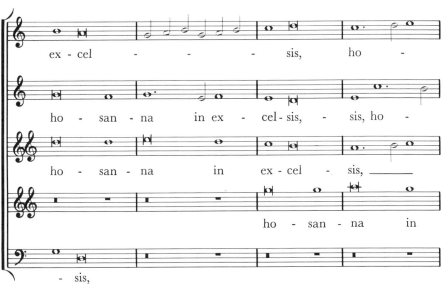

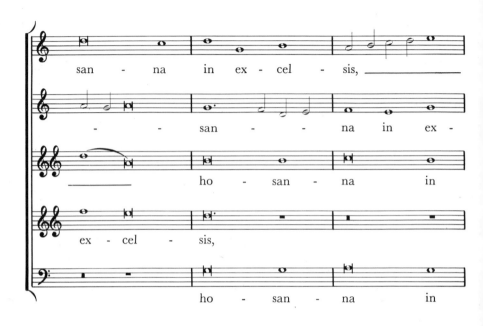

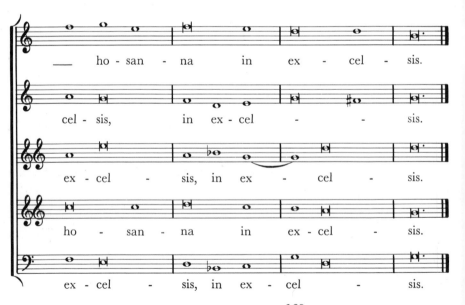

MASS: *Papae Marcelli*

Palestrina